GEOMETRIC
Pillows & Afghans

Simple geometry and dynamic colors make these five easy afghans and pillows pop as home accessories! All are created with only basic crochet stitches.

Stripes	2
Diagonals	6
Blocks	10
Dots	14
Squares	18
General Instructions	24
Basic Stitches	29
Yarn Information	31
Meet Melissa Leapman	32

LEISURE ARTS, INC.
Maumelle, Arkansas

EASY

Finished Size:
Afghan: 48" x 64" (122 cm x 162.5 cm)
Pillow: 16" (40.5 cm) square

SHOPPING LIST

Yarn (Bulky Weight)

[5 ounces, 153 yards
(140 grams, 140 meters) per skein]:

Afghan
- ☐ Off White - 8 skeins
- ☐ Dk Purple - 6 skeins

Pillow
- ☐ Off White - 2 skeins
- ☐ Dk Purple - 1 skein

Crochet Hook
- ☐ Size K (6.5 mm)
  or size needed for gauge

Additional Supplies
- ☐ 16" (40.5 cm) Square pillow form
- ☐ Yarn needle

STRIPES

GAUGE INFORMATION

13 dc = 5" (12.75 cm);
11 rows = 8" (20.25 cm)
One Square = 16" (40.5 cm)

Gauge Swatch: 5"w x 4¼"h
(12.75 cm x 10.75 cm)

With Off White, ch 15.

Row 1: Dc in fourth ch from hook **(3 skipped chs count as first dc)** and in each ch across: 13 dc.

Rows 2-6: Ch 3 **(counts as first dc)**, turn; dc in next dc and in each dc across.

Finish off.

AFGHAN

Square (Make 12)

With Off White, ch 44.

Row 1 (Right side)**:** Dc in fourth ch from hook **(3 skipped chs count as first dc)** and in each ch across: 42 dc.

Note: Loop a short piece of yarn around any stitch to mark Row 1 as **right** side.

Row 2: Ch 3 **(counts as first dc, now and throughout)**, turn; dc in next dc and in each dc across changing to Dk Purple in last dc ***(Fig. A)***.

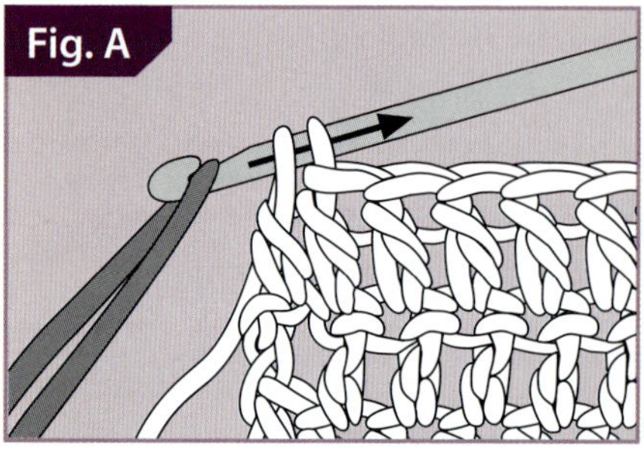

Row 3: Ch 3, turn; dc in next dc and in each dc across.

Row 4: Ch 3, turn; dc in next dc and in each dc across changing to Off White in last dc.

Row 5: Ch 3, turn; dc in next dc and in each dc across.

Row 6: Ch 3, turn; dc in next dc and in each dc across changing to Dk Purple in last dc.

Rows 7-22: Repeat Rows 3-6, 4 times; at end of Row 22, do **not** change to Dk Purple.

Finish off.

Assembly

With Off White and using Placement Diagram as a guide, sew Squares together, forming 3 vertical strips of 4 Squares each; then sew strips together.

PLACEMENT DIAGRAM

PILLOW
Square (Make 2)
Work same as Afghan, page 4.

Assembly

With **wrong** side of both pieces together and alternating direction of stripes on each side, sew 3 sides of Squares together; insert pillow form and sew remaining side closed.

EASY

Finished Size:
Afghan: 48" x 64" (122 cm x 162.5 cm)
Pillow: 16" (40.5 cm) square

SHOPPING LIST

Yarn (Bulky Weight)

[5 ounces, 155 yards
(140 grams, 142 meters) per skein]:

Afghan
- ☐ Black - 10 skeins
- ☐ White - 10 skeins

Pillow
- ☐ Black - 2 skeins
- ☐ White - 2 skeins

Crochet Hook
- ☐ Size K (6.5 mm)
    or size needed for gauge

Additional Supplies
- ☐ 16" (40.5 cm) Square pillow form
- ☐ Yarn needle

GAUGE INFORMATION

In pattern,

   11 sts and 12 rows = 4" (10 cm)

   One Square = 16" (40.5 cm)

Gauge Swatch: 4" (10 cm) square
With White, ch 12.

Row 1: Sc in second ch from hook and in each ch across: 11 sc.

Rows 2-12: Ch 1, turn; sc in each sc across.
Finish off.

STITCH GUIDE

BEGINNING DECREASE
  (uses first 2 sts)
YO, insert hook in first st, YO and pull up a loop (3 loops on hook), pull up a loop in next sc, YO and draw through all 4 loops on hook.

DECREASE (uses next 2 sts)
Pull up a loop in next sc (2 loops on hook), YO, insert hook in next st, YO and pull up a loop, YO and draw through all 4 loops on hook.

AFGHAN

Square (Make 12)

Row 1: With White, ch 2, 2 sc in second ch from hook: 2 sc.

Row 2 (Right side): Ch 1, turn; (hdc, sc) in first sc, (sc, hdc) in last sc: 4 sts.

Note: Loop a short piece of yarn around any stitch to mark Row 2 as **right** side.

Row 3: Ch 1, turn; (hdc, sc) in first hdc, sc in next 2 sc, (sc, hdc) in last hdc: 6 sts.

Rows 4-32: Ch 1, turn; (hdc, sc) in first hdc, sc in each sc across to last hdc, (sc, hdc) in last hdc: 64 sts.

Row 33: Ch 1, turn; (hdc, sc) in first hdc, sc in each sc across to last hdc, (sc, hdc) in last hdc changing to Black in last hdc made *(Fig. A)*: 66 sts.

Fig. A

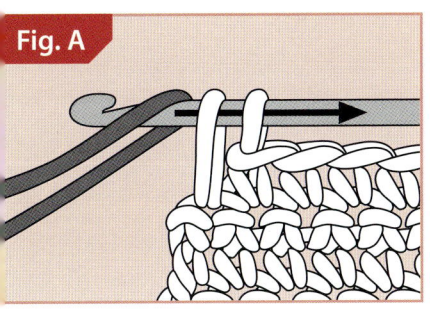

Rows 34-64: Ch 1, turn; work beginning decrease, sc in next sc and in each sc across to last 2 sts, decrease: 4 sts.

Row 65: Ch 1, turn; work beginning decrease, decrease: 2 sts.

Row 66: Ch 1, turn; pull up a loop in each of first 2 sts, YO and draw through all 3 loops on hook; finish off leaving a long end for sewing: one st.

Assembly

Using Placement Diagram as a guide, sew Squares together forming 3 vertical strips of 4 Squares each; then sew strips together in same manner.

PILLOW
Square (Make 2)
Work same as Afghan, page 8.

Assembly

With **wrong** sides together, sew 3 sides of Squares together; insert pillow form and sew remaining side closed.

PLACEMENT DIAGRAM

EASY

Finished Size:
Afghan: 50" x 66½" (127 cm x 169 cm)
Pillow: 16½" (42 cm) square

■ ■ ■ SHOPPING LIST ■ ■ ■

Yarn (Medium Weight)

[4.5 ounces, 247 yards
(127 grams, 225 meters) per skein]:

Afghan
- ☐ Peach - 6 skeins
- ☐ Grey - 6 skeins
- ☐ Green - 6 skeins

Pillow
- ☐ Peach **or** Green - 2 skeins
- ☐ Grey - 2 skeins

Crochet Hook
- ☐ Size M/N (9 mm)
  or size needed for gauge

Additional Supplies
- ☐ 16" (40.5 cm) Square pillow form
- ☐ Yarn needle

BLOCKS

Afghan is worked holding two strands of the same color yarn together.

GAUGE INFORMATION

10 dc and 5 rows = 4¼" (10 cm)
One Block = 16½" (42 cm)

Gauge Swatch:
4" (10 cm) square
With Peach, ch 12.
Row 1: Dc in fourth ch from hook **(3 skipped chs count as first dc)** and in each ch across: 10 dc.
Rows 2-5: Ch 3 **(counts as first dc)**, turn; dc in next dc and in each dc across.
Finish off.

AFGHAN

Block A (Make 4)
With Peach, ch 40.

Row 1 (Right side): Dc in fourth ch from hook **(3 skipped chs count as first dc)** and in each ch across: 38 dc.

Note: Loop a short piece of yarn around any stitch to mark Row 1 as **right** side and bottom edge.

Row 2: Ch 3 **(counts as first dc)**, turn; dc in next dc and in each dc across.

Repeat Row 2 until Block measures approximately 16" (40.5 cm) from beginning ch, ending by working a **right** side row; do **not** finish off.

Edging: Ch 1, do **not** turn; 2 sc in last dc of last row; work 36 sc evenly spaced across end of rows; working in free loops of beginning ch *(Fig. 1, page 27)*, 3 sc in first ch, sc in next 36 chs, 3 sc in next ch; work 36 sc evenly spaced across end of rows; working in dc across last row, 3 sc in first dc, sc in next 36 dc and in same dc as first sc; join with slip st to first sc, finish off: 156 sc.

Block B (Make 4)
With Grey, work same as Block A.

Block C (Make 4)
With Green, work same as Block A.

Assembly
With Grey and using Placement Diagram as a guide, whipstitch Blocks together *(Fig. 2, page 27)*, forming 3 vertical strips of 4 Blocks each; then whipstitch strips together.

PLACEMENT DIAGRAM

Edging
Rnd 1: With **right** side facing, Grey with sc in any corner *(see Joining With Sc, page 26)*; working from **left** to **right**, work reverse sc evenly around entire Afghan *(Figs. 3a-d, page 28)*; join with slip st to first sc, finish off.

PILLOW
Block A
Work same as Afghan Block A or C.

Block B
Work same as Afghan.

Assembly
With **wrong** sides and bottom edges together, matching sts and working through **both** thicknesses, join Grey with sc in any corner *(see Joining With Sc, page 26)*; working from **left** to **right**, work reverse sc evenly around *(Figs. 3a-d, page 28)* inserting pillow form before closing; join with slip st to first sc, finish off.

EASY

Finished Size:
Afghan: 49½" x 66" (125.5 cm x 167.5 cm)
Pillow: 16½" (42 cm) square

SHOPPING LIST

Yarn (Bulky Weight)
[3.5 ounces, 148 yards
(100 grams, 136 meters) per skein]:

Afghan
- ☐ Orange - 8 skeins
- ☐ Blue - 8 skeins

Pillow
- ☐ Orange - 2 skeins
- ☐ Blue - 2 skeins

Crochet Hook
- ☐ Size K (6.5 mm)
  or size needed for gauge

Additional Supplies
- ☐ 16" (40.5 cm) Square pillow form
- ☐ Yarn needle

DOTS

GAUGE INFORMATION

In pattern,
   12 dc and 6 rows = 4" (10 cm)
   One Square = 16½" (42 cm)
Gauge Swatch: 4" (10 cm) square
With Orange, ch 14.
Row 1: Dc in fourth ch from hook **(3 skipped chs count as first dc)** and in each ch across: 12 dc.
Rows 2-6: Ch 3 (**counts as first dc**), turn; dc in next dc and in each dc across.
Finish off.

Rows 2-4: Ch 3 (**counts as first dc, now and throughout**), turn; dc in next dc and in each dc across.

Row 5: Ch 3, turn; dc in next 18 dc changing to Blue in last dc made *(Fig. A)*, dc in next 10 dc changing to Orange in last dc made, dc in last 19 dc.

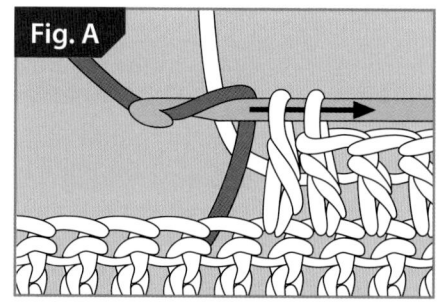
Fig. A

Rows 6-24: Follow Chart, page 17; at end of last row, do **not** finish off.

Edging: Ch 1, turn; 2 sc in first dc, sc in each dc across to last dc, 3 sc in last dc; working in end of rows, sc in first row, 2 sc in each of next 22 rows, sc in last row; working in free loops of beginning ch *(Fig. 1, page 27)*, 3 sc in first ch, sc in next 46 chs, 3 sc in next ch; working in

AFGHAN

Square A (Make 6)
With Orange, ch 50.

Row 1 (Right side): Dc in fourth ch from hook (**3 skipped chs count as first dc**) and in each ch across: 48 dc.

Note: Loop a short piece of yarn around any stitch to mark Row 1 as **right** side and bottom edge.

end of rows, sc in first row, 2 sc in each of next 22 rows, sc in last row and in same dc as first sc; join with slip st to first sc, finish off: 196 sc.

CHART

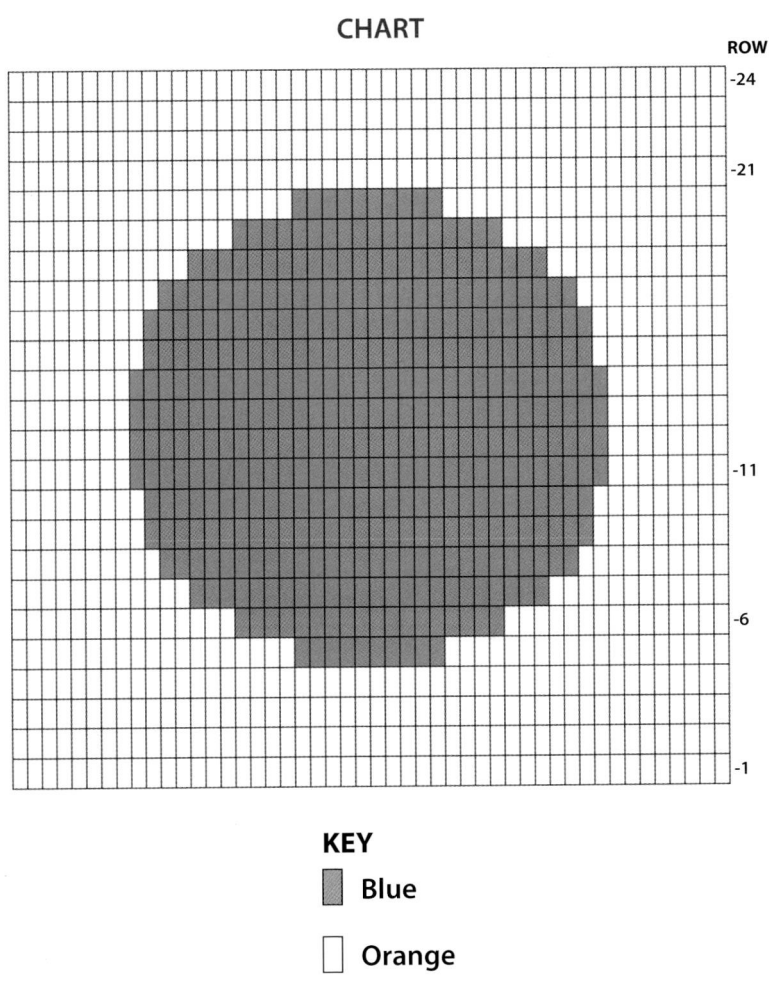

KEY
■ Blue
☐ Orange

Each rectangle represents one dc.

Continued on page 23.

EASY

Finished Size:
Afghan: 48" x 64" (122 cm x 162.5 cm)
Pillow: 16" (40.5 cm) square

SHOPPING LIST

Yarn (Bulky Weight)

[3.5 ounces, 120 yards
(100 grams, 109 meters) per skein]:

Afghan
- ☐ Natural - 10 skeins
- ☐ Yellow - 10 skeins

Pillow
- ☐ Natural - 2 skeins
- ☐ Yellow - 2 skeins

Crochet Hook
- ☐ Size K (6.5 mm)
  or size needed for gauge

Additional Supplies
- ☐ 16" (40.5 cm) Square pillow form
- ☐ Yarn needle

SQUARES

GAUGE INFORMATION

13 dc = 4½" (11.5 cm);

  6 rnds = 4" (10 cm)

  One Square = 16" (40.5 cm)

Gauge Swatch:

  4¼" (10.75 cm) square
Work same as Square A through Rnd 3: 44 dc.

AFGHAN

Square A (Make 6)

With Natural, ch 4; join with slip st to form a ring.

Rnd 1 (Right side): Ch 3 **(counts as first dc, now and throughout)**, 11 dc in ring; join with slip st to first dc: 12 dc.

Note: Loop a short piece of yarn around any stitch to mark Rnd 1 as **right** side.

Rnd 2: Ch 3, 4 dc in same st as joining, dc in next 2 dc, (5 dc in next dc, dc in next 2 dc) around; join with slip st to first dc: 28 dc.

Rnd 3: Ch 3, dc in next dc, 5 dc in next dc, (dc in next 6 dc, 5 dc in next dc) 3 times, dc in last 4 dc; join with slip st to first dc: 44 dc.

Rnd 4: Ch 3, dc in next 3 dc, 5 dc in next dc, (dc in next 10 dc, 5 dc in next dc) 3 times, dc in last 6 dc; join with slip st to first dc: 60 dc.

Rnd 5: Ch 3, dc in next 5 dc, 5 dc in next dc, (dc in next 14 dc, 5 dc in next dc) 3 times, dc in last 8 dc; join with slip st to first dc: 76 dc.

Rnd 6: Ch 3, dc in next 7 dc, 5 dc in next dc, (dc in next 18 dc, 5 dc in next dc) 3 times, dc in last 10 dc; join with slip st to first dc changing to Yellow *(Fig. A)*: 92 dc.

Fig. A

Rnd 7: Ch 3, dc in next 9 dc, 5 dc in next dc, (dc in next 22 dc, 5 dc in next dc) 3 times, dc in last 12 dc; join with slip st to first dc: 108 dc.

Rnd 8: Ch 3, dc in next 11 dc, 5 dc in next dc, (dc in next 26 dc, 5 dc in next dc) 3 times, dc in last 14 dc; join with slip st to first dc: 124 dc.

Rnd 9: Ch 3, dc in next 13 dc, 5 dc in next dc, (dc in next 30 dc, 5 dc in next dc) 3 times, dc in last 16 dc; join with slip st to first dc: 140 dc.

Rnd 10: Ch 3, dc in next 15 dc, 5 dc in next dc, (dc in next 34 dc, 5 dc in next dc) 3 times, dc in last 18 dc; join with slip st to first dc: 156 dc.

Rnd 11: Ch 3, dc in next 17 dc, 5 dc in next dc, (dc in next 38 dc, 5 dc in next dc) 3 times, dc in last 20 dc; join with slip st to first dc: 172 dc.

Rnd 12: Ch 3, dc in next 19 dc, 5 dc in next dc, (dc in next 42 dc, 5 dc in next dc) 3 times, dc in last 22 dc; join with slip st to first dc, finish off: 188 dc.

Square B (Make 6)
With Yellow, work same as Square A, page 20, through Rnd 6, changing to Natural at end of Rnd 6: 92 dc.

Rnds 7-12: Complete same as Square A: 188 dc.

Assembly

With Yellow and using Placement Diagram as a guide, whipstitch Squares together *(Fig. 2, page 27)*, forming 3 vertical strips of 4 Squares each; then whipstitch strips together.

PLACEMENT DIAGRAM

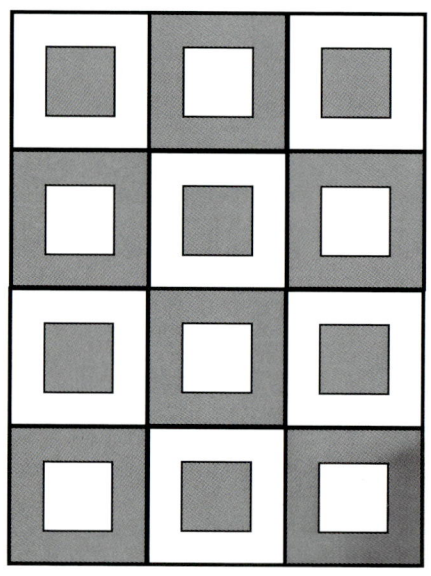

PILLOW
Square A
Work same as Afghan, page 20.

Square B
Work same as Afghan.

Assembly

With **wrong** sides together, whipstitch 3 sides of Squares together *(Fig. 2, page 27)* insert pillow form and whipstitch remaining side closed.

DOTS Continued from page 17.

Square B (Make 6)
Work same as Square A, page 16, reversing colors.

Assembly
With Blue and using Placement Diagram as a guide, whipstitch Squares together *(Fig. 2, page 27)*, forming 3 vertical strips of 4 Squares each; then whipstitch strips together.

PLACEMENT DIAGRAM

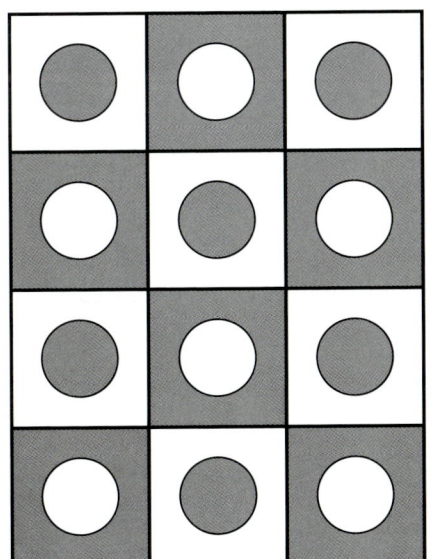

PILLOW
Square A
Work same as Afghan, page 16.

Square B
Work same as Afghan.

Assembly
With **wrong** sides and bottom edges together, whipstitch 3 sides of Squares together *(Fig. 2, page 27)*; insert pillow form and whipstitch remaining side closed.

GENERAL INSTRUCTIONS

ABBREVIATIONS

ch(s)	chain(s)
cm	centimeters
dc	double crochet(s)
hdc	half double crochet(s)
mm	millimeters
Rnd(s)	Round(s)
sc	single crochet(s)
st(s)	stitch(es)
YO	yarn over

SYMBOLS & TERMS

★ — work instructions following ★ as many **more** times as indicated in addition to the first time.

( ) or [ ] — work enclosed instructions **as many** times as specified by the number immediately following **or** work all enclosed instructions in the stitch or space indicated **or** contains explanatory remarks.

colon (:) — the number(s) given after a colon at the end of a row or round denote(s) the number of stitches or spaces you should have on that row or round.

CROCHET HOOKS														
U.S.	B-1	C-2	D-3	E-4	F-5	G-6	7	H-8	I-9	J-10	K-10½	L-11	M/N-13	N/P-15	P/Q	Q	S
Metric - mm	2.25	2.75	3.25	3.5	3.75	4	4.5	5	5.5	6	6.5	8	9	10	15	16	19

CROCHET TERMINOLOGY	
UNITED STATES	INTERNATIONAL
slip stitch (slip st) =	single crochet (sc)
single crochet (sc) =	double crochet (dc)
half double crochet (hdc) =	half treble crochet (htr)
double crochet (dc) =	treble crochet (tr)
treble crochet (tr) =	double treble crochet (dtr)
double treble crochet (dtr) =	triple treble crochet (ttr)
triple treble crochet (tr tr) =	quadruple treble crochet (qtr)
skip =	miss

●○○○ BEGINNER	Projects for first-time crocheters using basic stitches. Minimal shaping.
●●○○ EASY	Projects using yarn with basic stitches, repetitive stitch patterns, simple color changes, and simple shaping and finishing.
●●●○ INTERMEDIATE	Projects using a variety of techniques, such as basic lace patterns or color patterns, mid-level shaping and finishing.
●●●● EXPERIENCED	Projects with intricate stitch patterns, techniques and dimension, such as non-repeating patterns, multi-color techniques, fine threads, small hooks, detailed shaping and refined finishing.

Yarn Weight Symbol & Names	LACE 0	SUPER FINE 1	FINE 2	LIGHT 3	MEDIUM 4	BULKY 5	SUPER BULKY 6	JUMBO 7
Type of Yarns in Category	Fingering, size 10 crochet thread	Sock, Fingering, Baby	Sport, Baby	DK, Light Worsted	Worsted, Afghan, Aran	Chunky, Craft, Rug	Super Bulky, Roving	Jumbo, Roving
Crochet Gauge* Ranges in Single Crochet to 4" (10 cm)	32-42 sts**	21-32 sts	16-20 sts	12-17 sts	11-14 sts	8-11 sts	6-9 sts	5 sts and fewer
Advised Hook Size Range	Steel*** 6 to 8, Regular hook B-1	B-1 to E-4	E-4 to 7	7 to I-9	I-9 to K-10½	K-10½ to M/N-13	M/N-13 to Q	Q and larger

*GUIDELINES ONLY: The chart above reflects the most commonly used gauges and hook sizes for specific yarn categories.

** Lace weight yarns are usually crocheted with larger hooks to create lacy openwork patterns. Accordingly, a gauge range is difficult to determine. Always follow the gauge stated in your pattern.

*** Steel crochet hooks are sized differently from regular hooks–the higher the number, the smaller the hook, which is the reverse of regular hook sizing.

GAUGE

Exact gauge is **essential** for proper size. Before beginning your Afghan and Pillow, make the sample swatch given in the individual instructions in the yarn and hook specified. After completing the swatch, measure it, counting your stitches and rows or rounds carefully. If your swatch is larger or smaller than specified, **make another, changing hook size to get the correct gauge**. Keep trying until you find the size hook that will give you the specified gauge.

HINTS

As in all crocheted pieces, good finishing techniques make a big difference in the quality of the piece. Make a habit of taking care of loose ends as you work. Thread a yarn needle with the yarn end. With **wrong** side facing, weave the needle through several stitches, then reverse the direction and weave it back through several stitches. When ends are secure, clip them off close to work.

JOINING WITH SC

When instructed to join with sc, begin with a slip knot on hook. Insert hook in the stitch or space indicated, YO and pull up a loop, YO and draw through both loops on hook.

FREE LOOPS OF A CHAIN

When instructed to work in free loops of a chain, work in loop indicated by arrow *(Fig. 1)*.

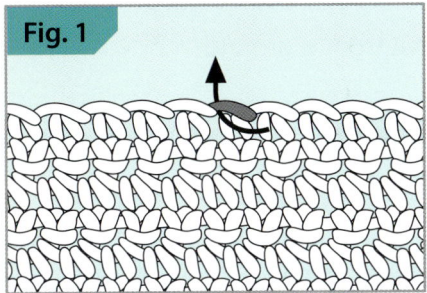

WHIPSTITCH

Place two pieces with **wrong** sides together. Beginning in center stitch of corner, sew through both pieces once to secure the beginning of the seam, leaving an ample yarn end to weave in later. Insert the needle from **front** to **back** through **both** loops of **both** pieces *(Fig. 2)*. Bring the needle around and insert it from **front** to **back** through next loops of both pieces. Continue in this manner across to center stitch of next corner, keeping the sewing yarn fairly loose.

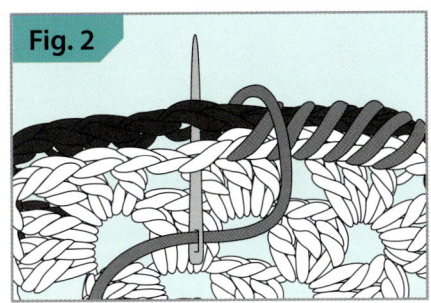

REVERSE SINGLE CROCHET

Working from **left** to **right**, ★ insert hook in stitch to right of hook *(Fig. 3a)*, YO and draw through, under and to the left of loop on hook (2 loops on hook) *(Fig. 3b)*, YO and draw through both loops on hook *(Fig. 3c)* (**reverse sc made,** *Fig. 3d)*; repeat from ★ around.

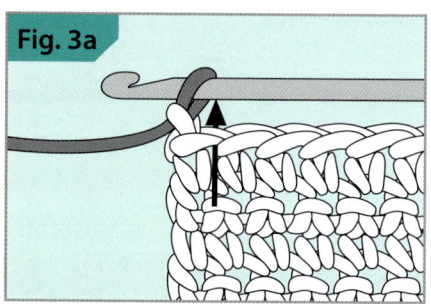
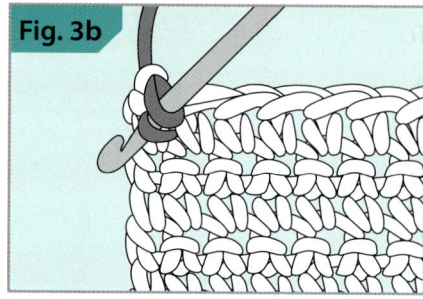
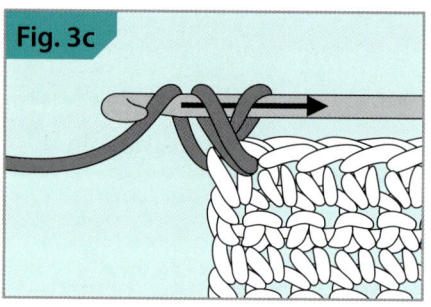
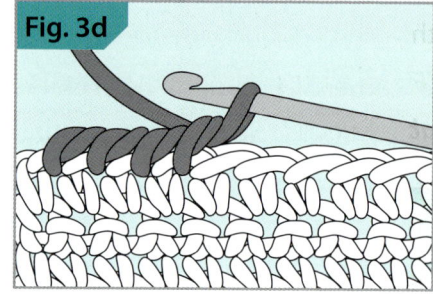

BASIC STITCHES

CHAIN

To work a chain stitch, begin with a slip knot on the hook. Bring the yarn over the hook from **back** to **front**, catching the yarn with the hook and turning the hook slightly toward you to keep the yarn from slipping off. Draw the yarn through the slip knot *(Fig. 4)* (**first chain stitch made,** *abbreviated ch*).

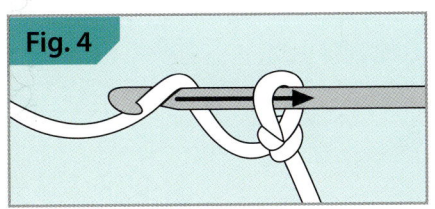

Fig. 4

SLIP STITCH

To work a slip stitch, insert hook in the stitch indicated, YO and draw through stitch **and** through loop on hook *(Fig. 5)* (**slip stitch made,** *abbreviated slip st*).

Fig. 5

SINGLE CROCHET

Insert hook in the stitch indicated, YO and pull up a loop, YO and draw through both loops on the hook *(Fig. 6)* (**single crochet made,** *abbreviated sc*).

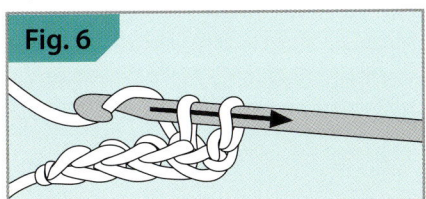

Fig. 6

HALF DOUBLE CROCHET

YO, insert hook in the stitch indicated, YO and pull up a loop, YO and draw through all 3 loops on hook *(Fig. 7)* (**half double crochet made,** *abbreviated hdc*).

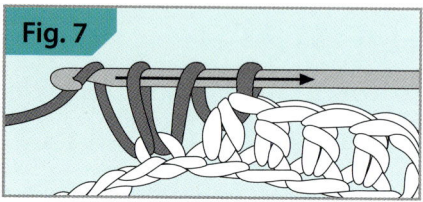

DOUBLE CROCHET

YO, insert hook in the stitch indicated, YO and pull up a loop (3 loops on hook), YO and draw through 2 loops on hook *(Fig. 8a)*, YO and draw through remaining 2 loops on hook *(Fig. 8b)* (**double crochet made,** *abbreviated dc*).

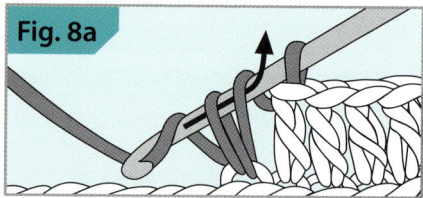 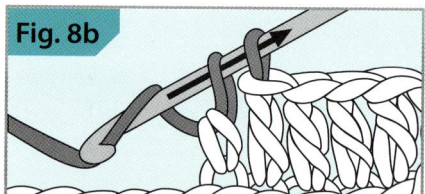

YARN INFORMATION

The Afghans & Pillows in this book were made using various weights of yarn. Any brand of the specified weight of yarn may be used. It is best to refer to the yardage/meters when determining how many ball or skeins to purchase. Remember, to arrive at the finished size, it is the GAUGE/TENSION that is important, not the brand of yarn.

For your convenience, listed below are the specific yarns used to create our photography models. Because yarn manufacturers make frequent changes in their product lines, you may sometimes find it necessary to use a substitute yarn or to search for the discontinued product at alternate suppliers (locally or online).

STRIPES
Lion Brand® Wool-Ease® Chunky
Off White - #402 Wheat
Dk Purple - #144 Eggplant

DIAGONALS
Bernat® Softee® Baby Chunky™
Black - #96017 Nighty Night
White - #96001 Fluffy Cloud White

DOTS
Patons® Shetland Chunky™
Orange - #78628 Fiesta
Blue - #78743 Mallard

BLOCKS
Red Heart® Babyhugs™ Medium
Peach - #4258 Peachie
Grey - #4410 Dolphin
Green - #4562 Aloe

SQUARES
Patons® Classic Wool Roving™
Natural - #77010 Natural
Yellow - #77615 Yellow

MEET THE DESIGNER
Melissa Leapman

With more than 800 knit and crochet designs in print, Melissa Leapman is one of the most widely published American designers working today.

She began her design career by freelancing for leading ready-to-wear design houses in New York City. She also created designs to help top yarn companies promote their new and existing yarns each season. Her ability to quickly develop fully envisioned garments put her skills in great demand.

Through the years, Leisure Arts has published more than 40 books of Melissa's fabulous designs. Melissa is also the host of several Leisure Arts DVDs in the best-selling teach-yourself series, "I Can't Believe I'm Knitting" and "I Can't Believe I'm Crocheting."

Nationally, her designs have been featured in numerous magazines, and her workshops on knitting and crochet are consistently popular with crafters of all skill levels. She has taught at major events such as STITCHES, Vogue Knitting LIVE, and The Knitting Guild Association conferences, as well as at hundreds of yarn shops and local guild events across the country.

To find more of Melissa's exciting designs, visit LeisureArts.com, "like" Melissa's Facebook page, and join her group (Melissa Leapman Rocks) on Ravelry.com.

Afghans & Pillows made and instructions tested by Raymelle Greening and Barbara Schou.

We have made every effort to ensure that these instructions are accurate and complete. We cannot, however, be responsible for human error, typographical mistakes, or variations in individual work.

Production Team: Instructional/Technical Editor - Linda A. Daley; Editorial Writer - Susan Frantz Wiles; Senior Graphic Artist - Lora Puls; Graphic Artist - Leia Morshedi; Photo Stylist - Lori Wenger; and Photographer - Jason Masters.

Copyright © 2016 by Leisure Arts, Inc., 104 Champs Blvd., STE 100, Maumelle, AR 72113-6738, www.leisurearts.com. All rights reserved. This publication is protected under federal copyright laws. Reproduction or distribution of this publication or any other Leisure Arts publication, including publications which are out of print, is prohibited unless specifically authorized. This includes, but is not limited to, any form of reproduction or distribution on or through the Internet, including posting, scanning, or e-mail transmission.